Your
Horoscope
2020

....

Taurus

D1513504

Your Horoscope 2020

· · · · · · · · · · · · · · · ·

Taurus

21st April - 21st May

igloobooks

Published in 2019
by Igloo Books Ltd
Cottage Farm
Sywell
NN6 0BJ
www.igloobooks.com

Copyright © 2018 Igloo Books Ltd
Igloo Books is an imprint of Bonnier Books UK

0819 001.01
2 4 6 8 10 9 7 5 3 1
ISBN 978-1-78905-719-5

Written by Belinda Campbell and Denise Evans

Cover design by Dave Chapman
Edited by Bobby Newlyn-Jones

Printed and manufactured in China

CONTENTS

. . . .

1. Introduction **7**

2. The Character of the Bull **9**

3. Love **15**

4. Family and Friends **22**

5. Money and Career **24**

6. Health and Wellbeing **27**

7. 2020 Diary Pages **31**

8. People Who Share Your Star Sign **137**

INTRODUCTION
. . . .

This horoscope has been specifically created to allow
you to get the most from astrological patterns and
the way they have a bearing on not only your zodiac
sign, but nuances within it. Using the diary section
of the book you can read about the influences and
possibilities of each and every day of the year. It will
be possible for you to see when you are likely to be
cheerful and happy or those times when your nature
is in retreat and you will be more circumspect. The
diary will help to give you a feel for the specific
'cycles' of astrology and the way they can subtly
change your day-to-day life.

THE CHARACTER OF THE BULL

....

Steady and grounded, Taurus is a fixed Earth sign that
the rest of the zodiac can surely rely on. Slow and
steady is how this Bull wins the race. Those who have
a Taurean in their life should learn to not expect fast
results. But boy, when a Taurean delivers, it is likely to
be a stunning result. Taurus is known for being one
of the most multitalented signs in the zodiac calendar,
with a keen eye for the aesthetic. Some of the best
artists, makers, writers and creators the world has ever
known have been Taureans, such as Salvador Dalí and
William Shakespeare.

Lovers of the finer things in life, Taureans may want to
surround themselves with beautiful soft furnishings,
sparkling jewellery, alluring artwork and other riches.
Likewise, Taureans will gorge themselves on equally fine
wines and delicious foods. The lure of beautiful things
can be constant for Taureans, and whilst this can feel
like a cruel fate when money is not free flowing, it can
be an added motivation for doggedly pursuing their
goals. Perseverance, after all, is what this sign is also
best known for. The Taurean love of beauty does not
always stop with material things. This springtime sign
has a deep connection with Mother Earth. Hiking and
working outdoors to enjoy the beauty of the world or
finding ways to preserve and protect nature's wonders
can be integral to Taureans. The associated colour
for Taurus is green and whilst this may be linked

to a love of Earth, it can also be an indicator of a green-eyed monster that lies within. Possession is a key characteristic of the Bull and whilst this usually relates to material objects, Taureans can sometimes be guilty of treating their loved ones as possessions too. Jealousy, superficiality and stubbornness are the potential downsides of the talented, nurturing and tenacious Taurean.

THE BULL

Strong and masculine, the Bull inside of Taurus has plenty of charge and direction – there's a reason why everyone aims for the bullseye! The Bull is capable of charging when necessary, similarly Taureans can roll up their sleeves and deliver solid and fast results when life demands it. However, like the Bull, Taureans are more suited to a slower pace of life. Stopping to smell the flowers, taking time to relax in green pastures; this instinct of appreciating Mother Earth should be indulged whenever possible. This sign has an utmost appreciation for the finer things in life, but too often this is translated into material objects and wealth alone. What Taureans value and benefit from most is a long meander through woodlands or reading a good book in the park. Taureans can be accused of being bullish or stubborn, particularly when change is happening that they are uncomfortable with, or if it feels too great or sudden. In ancient Greek mythology, Zeus transformed himself into a white bull and whisked his love Europa to Crete. Zeus's bull has many similarities with Taureans; romantic, tenacious, sometimes possessive and often mystical. Ultimately, the friends and family of a Taurean should feel safe with the Bull by their side, an utmost nurturing and protective symbol that slowly but steadily provides for loved ones.

VENUS

Venus is named after the Roman goddess of love and beauty, so it is no surprise that these very two things govern Taurus. Taureans can happily spend a night at the theatre, ballet or opera, nestled in plush, red velvet seats and revelling in some of the finest displays of beauty and culture with a glass of fine wine. Slaves to their senses, Taureans can take immense pleasure in music, art, dining and, last but not least, physical activities. Encouraged by Venus, tactile Taureans can have a reputation for being sensual lovers. Considered to be some of the most attractive people, guided by their desires and ruled by the planet of love, romance is likely to play a huge role in the life of a Taurean.

ELEMENTS, MODES AND POLARITIES

Each sign is made up of a unique combination of three defining groups: elements, modes and polarities. Each of these defining parts can manifest themselves in good and bad ways and none should be seen to be a positive or a negative – including the polarities! Just like a jigsaw puzzle, piecing these groups together can help illuminate why each sign has certain characteristics and help us find a balance.

ELEMENTS

Fire: Dynamic and adventurous, signs with Fire in them can be extrovert characters that others are naturally drawn to because of the positive light they give off and their high levels of energy and confidence.

Earth: Signs with the Earth element are steady and driven with their ambitions and make for a solid friend, parent or partner due to their grounded influence and nurturing nature.

Air: The invisible element that influences each of the other elements significantly, Air signs will provide much needed perspective to others with their fair thinking, verbal skills and key ideas.

Water: Warm in the shallows and freezing as ice. This mysterious element is essential to the growth of everything around it, through its emotional depth and empathy.

MODES

Cardinal: Pioneers of the calendar, cardinal signs jump-start each season and are the energetic go-getters.

Fixed: Marking the middle of the calendar, fixed signs firmly denote and value steadiness and reliability.

Mutable: As the seasons end, the mutable signs adapt and give themselves over gladly to the promise of change.

POLARITIES

Positive: Typically extroverted, positive signs take physical action and embrace outside stimulus in their life.

Negative: Usually introverted, negative signs value emotional development and experiencing life from the inward out.

TAURUS IN BRIEF

The table below shows the key attributes of Taureans.
Use it for quick reference and to understand more about
this fascinating sign.

SYMBOL	RULING PLANET	MODE	ELEMENT	HOUSE
♉	♀	⊟	▽	♊
The Bull	Venus	Fixed	Earth	Second

COLOUR	BODY PART	POLARITY	GENDER	POLAR SIGN
		⊖	♀	♏
Green	Neck and throat	Negative	Feminine	Scorpio

LOVE

. . . .

The slow and steady nature of Taureans means that quick-fire love affairs are unlikely. Instead, they are more likely to find romance blossoming from a friendship, or pursue someone who has been on the outskirts of their life for a while. A sense of security is important to Taureans for their relationships to succeed. An insecure Taurean can turn into a jealous creature that is guilty of suffocating a relationship in a misguided effort to greedily possess a partner. Perhaps the most important lesson for this tempered Bull to learn is how to share a partner's time rather then attempt to dominate it. This is not always an easy task for Taureans, particularly if they come from a small family and are less used to sharing their loved ones. Yet it's an important lesson to practise regularly to keep significant others happy. As with most things, sharing can be easier said than done. Communicating emotions is essential to any successful relationship, and will lead to deeper affection between Taureans and their loved ones.

An ideal partner for a Taurean is one that feeds both the desires and the stomach! Food is essential to the happiness of a Taurean, so the trick to keeping the relationship sweet may be to keep those snack drawers well stocked. A partner who cooks is one that a Taurean will be more inclined to try and keep hold of. Whilst Taureans love to be doted on and thrive on affection from their spouse, they should not be pandered to. A good partner for a Taurean should maintain a level of autonomy and not be tempted to indulge in letting their lover take ownership over them – even if it makes for an easier life! A Taurean's equal should fight to keep their individuality, but also display patience and love. In return, a Taurean will show fierce loyalty and love, for better or for worse.

ARIES: COMPATIBILITY 3/5

The Bull and the Ram may look like two headstrong individuals doomed to clash, but they actually have the potential for a sensual relationship. Whilst their passions for each other are intense, this couple will need to keep a reign on their potential stubbornness and desire to win in order to form a lasting relationship outside of the sheets. The Taurean can be guilty of possessiveness, which the free spirited Arean may struggle with. However, with a joint love of nature and being outdoors, this passionate duo could find their Eden together.

TAURUS: COMPATIBILITY 4/5

This love can be one for the ages. When a Taurean falls for a Taurean, it may be slow and steady as is their usual way or it can be love, and lust, at first sight. These two romantics will shower each other with affection and reciprocate the dedication and loyalty that each deserves. Not one to give up, both Bulls will stand by the other through thick and thin. Should they not see eye to eye, these two are capable of fighting with terrifying passion but will hopefully find that making up is always more fun.

GEMINI: COMPATIBILITY 2/5

Three may prove to be a crowd. The duality of a Geminian, characterised in their Twin symbol, can make a Taurean feel uneasy in starting a romantic relationship with this sign. The Earth sign of Taurus mixed with airy Gemini may not be an easy joining, but if Taurus can budge on their fixed ways then love could grow happily here. Gemini's good communication skills will mean that they should hopefully understand quickly the needs of a Taurus and provide the love and security that Taureans crave in a partner. Communication, trust and flexibility should be this couple's mantra.

CANCER: COMPATIBILITY 5/5

Placed two positions apart on the zodiac calendar, a Cancerian and Taurean share a bond that can feel like home. The Cancerian's frequent displays of love are deep and clear, like two names carved into a tree! The intensity of the Taurean's affection, mixed with the Cancerian's head-over-heels approach, can see these two lovers running to the altar and settling down with babies – not always in that order. Here are two signs that will do anything for each other, and will usually prefer their own little party of two.

LEO: COMPATIBILITY 3/5

Leo is ruled by the Sun and Taurus by Venus; this star and planet are never further away than 48 degrees from each other. The love that these two share is solidified in their sometimes-stubborn commitment to one another.

The Lion and Bull are both fixed signs and this can be their undoing in a long-term relationship when neither one is willing to compromise. Both the Lion and Bull will shower each other with affection and admiration, and will boost each other's self-esteem and be a positive influence in their careers. This couple should just be careful to not let their egos get in the way.

VIRGO: COMPATIBILITY 3/5

A Taurean and Virgoan can make for a real power couple. The Taurean's dogged approach to fulfilling goals and the Virgoan's practical and busy mind will see this pair securing a successful future together. The Virgoan can appear overly critical and may end up hurting the Bull's feelings unintentionally. Ruled by Mercury, the planet of communication, the Virgoan can be very attuned to the Taurean's needs and will try to fix any problems within the relationship. These two Earth signs will likely share many things in common and can form lifelong companionships, even if a whirlwind romance isn't in the stars.

LIBRA: COMPATIBILITY 4/5

Both ruled by the planet Venus, the love that a Taurean and Libran share can be a thing of beauty. Their shared appreciation of culture and aesthetics will have romance blooming quickly. Wedding bells will ring in both the Taurean and Libran's ears, and planning for the big day will begin sooner rather than later. The Libran's airy indecisiveness can be a point of contention for the grounded Taurean, and these two won't be without their disagreements. However, the Libran's diplomacy will help to resolve issues and have them striving for harmony once more.

SCORPIO: COMPATIBILITY 5/5

Scorpio and Taurus are each other's opposites on the zodiac calendar, so therefore cosmically share a special relationship both in their differences and similarities. The element of Taurus is Earth and Scorpio's is Water, which usually will mean that both partners will provide something that the other desperately needs. Love and passion are both driving forces for these two. Scorpio has the reputation for being the sexiest of signs and Taurus the most beautiful, so a physical relationship should be strong here. Whilst this couple will no doubt enjoy each other's bodies immensely, their tendencies towards possession and jealousy will need to be kept in check.

SAGITTARIUS: COMPATIBILITY 2/5

A Sagittarian is ruled by the planet Jupiter, which is associated with luck – something that a Taurean doesn't always believe in. Whilst the Sagittarian values new experiences, the Taurean prefers familiar, safer comforts. The biggest struggle that this Fire and Earth couple may have is the Sagittarian's need for freedom, and the Taurean's tendency towards possessiveness with a partner. A claustrophobic atmosphere should be avoided, and freedom actively given in this relationship. They must learn from one another; both by admiring the

faster gallop of the Centaur, and equally by appreciating
the steady plod of the Bull.

CAPRICORN: COMPATIBILITY 3/5

A Capricornian and Taurean in love are loyal and true
to each other. These two Earth signs value hard work,
and are driven by their need to enjoy the fruits of their
labours. The home that these two could build together
will likely be full of beautiful and expensive objects,
with a couple of prized cars jewelling the garage. Whilst
both will have dreams of marriage, the Capricornian is
the more traditional one and will probably approach the
subject first. The Taurean should try to inject joy and fun
into the relationship to teach the Capricornian how to
enjoy the lighter side of life.

AQUARIUS: COMPATIBILITY 1/5

A Taurean and Aquarian aren't an obvious match on
paper, and it's unlikely they will be paired on a dating
website. The core differences between these two makes
a romantic spark unlikely, but should not be ruled out.
The Aquarian is partly ruled by the planet Uranus,
symbolising rebellion and change – often the Taurean's
worst nightmare. For the easy life-seeking Taurean who
likes what they know, the travel-lusting Aquarian can be
hard to keep up with. These two signs are both fixed and
have the potential to make each other stronger if they
remain open to change.

PISCES: COMPATIBILITY 3/5

A Taurean and Piscean are capable of having a highly sympathetic and understanding love together. The practical-minded Taurean should encourage the dreamy Piscean to live out fantasies and work hard, for everyone's benefit. In return, the Piscean will shower the Taurean in waves of love and gratitude for all the support and encouragement. However, the Piscean would be wise to not saturate the relationship emotionally and spoil the Taurean. With the Piscean being a Water sign, the Taurean can feel the nourishing effects this sign has on its Earth element, and the life that these two can grow together is one well worth living.

FAMILY AND FRIENDS

. . . .

Just as Taureans are dedicated to sticking to their goals, the same steadfast dedication is given to maintaining relationships with friends and family. Taureans want to see loved ones succeed, and will try to offer unfailing support mentally, physically and financially if they can. Positioned under the second house in the zodiac calendar, Taurus has a strong influence with possessions and money. Taureans are not ones to spend all their hard-earned wealth on just themselves, instead they are likely to want to share their fortunes with loved ones. From picking up a cheque for dinner to paying for extracurricular activities for their children, Taureans are generous with their love, time and money.

A Taurean home will clearly display signs of success, wealth and a love for beautiful and opulent design. From decorative throws and pillows, to the artwork hanging on the walls (that may or may not be a Taurean original), to the grand piano taking centre stage, the Taurean home will likely be a stunning display of the beauty in life. Beauty-loving Librans and homemaking Cancerians will value the stylish home that Taureans are capable of building, and can provide some of the most appreciative and kindred of friendships or relatives.

A key characteristic of Taureans is their focus on possession, which can lead them to become workaholics in their desire to be the affluent provider for their family

FAMILY AND FRIENDS
· · · · · · · · · · · · · · · ·

When it comes to family, it's important for Taureans to remember that whom they are providing for is more important than what they are providing. Despite their weakness toward possession, what Taureans are more reliably known for is their unmoving loyalty and stability, both key attributes for building a happy family home. If a Taurean befriends or is related to another Taurean, their relationship will have the strong bones for forming some of the most reliable and steady relationships that the zodiac calendar knows.

Be careful of upsetting Taureans because they can hold a grudge for years and years. They would do well to learn to forgive any friends and family they feel have done them an injustice, if they want to keep that person in their life. Taureans should ask themselves this question: is it more important to hold on to this grudge or to hold on to this relationship? Taureans choose their friendships wisely and will usually be unwilling to let go of their investment in it, even if the friendship has soured or become too toxic to remain close. Taureans should learn to live and let live, and move forwards from any disagreements that they have with their family and friends. If a Taurean chooses to keep a friendship after a falling out, it should be based on forgiveness with an unclouded look towards a happier, shared future.

MONEY AND CAREERS

· · · · · · · · · · · · · · · · · ·

Being a particular star sign will not dictate certain types of career, but it can help identify potential areas for thriving in. Conversely, to succeed in the workplace, it is just as important to understand strengths and weaknesses to achieve career and financial goals.

The mode of Taurus is fixed, rather than cardinal or mutable, which in career terms can mean that once Taureans decide what their career path is, they will stubbornly stick with it until they achieve their goal ambitions. Which career path to take may not always be clear, particularly as they are known for being multitalented. Whilst a career choice may be undecided, belonging to the second house in the zodiac calendar representing wealth will mean that dreams of money and fortune will no doubt be a driving force for all Taureans. A career in finance, such as investment banking, could be a satisfying job, as they will enjoy watching their investments grow over time. High-risk decisions won't be appealing to Taureans. Rather, a steadfast investment is something that will likely attract them to parting with their hard-earned money.

Whilst Taureans may be naturally good at a job in finance, the more negative characteristics associated with this sign, such as greed and being overly materialistic, may mean that this avenue is best avoided to help keep these traits at bay. A more grounded career, influenced by this sign's Earth element, may be complementary to a happy work life. The gradual and sustainable process of growing plants or vegetables lends itself to the slow-paced Taurean, so perhaps a career in horticulture would be well suited. Taureans' appreciation of beauty may lead to work in conservation, appealing to their nurturing side and their love of Mother Earth. Whether it is through full-time work or a leisurely activity, being in nature will have a positive and calming effect, and offer balance and perspective.

Ruled by Venus, the planet of beauty, the sign of Taurus has great potential with pursuing a career in the arts. Some of the best-known artists, including Salvador Dalí and William Shakespeare, are Taureans. Taureans strongly value security, and might struggle with the uncertainty of success, financial or otherwise, that a life in the arts can offer. This dislike for unsteady work and working for no immediate money are things that arty Taureans will need to overcome. However, their determination to hone their craft by stubbornly working towards their goals day by day can mean the bright lights of fame and success will be the ultimate pay-off. Taureans are known for not just appreciating beauty but also for being beautiful themselves, so perhaps a career in acting or fashion, like Taurean supermodel Gigi Hadid, may prove fulfilling.

As with family, colleagues cannot be chosen. Therefore, it can be advantageous to use star signs to learn about their key characteristics and discover the best ways of working together. As co-workers, Leonians can have a positive influence on Taureans by encouraging them to make bolder choices. However, Taureans may find

Leonians difficult bosses, as neither the Bull nor the Lion is likely to admit defeat graciously. Taureans are multitalented in the workplace, and share many skills with other signs; from their problem-solving initiative that links them with practical Virgoans, to the resolute ambition they share with desirous Scorpians. These appealing attributes, together with their calm and patient nature, make Taureans liked and valued by their colleagues.

HEALTH AND WELLBEING

Being a lover of the finest food and drink, Taureans can sometimes struggle with keeping their weight down. Not ones to deny themselves the luxury of eating out at fine restaurants, those calories can add up as high as their bill. And what's dinner without dessert? By making more meals from scratch at home, Taureans will be more aware of the ingredients going into their favourite foods. Taureans are known for their pre-planning and organisation skills. By utilising these positive traits in the kitchen, Taureans can prepare healthy meals ahead of time, and ensure that they are eating a more balanced diet.

Taurus rules the throat and neck and, like the Bull, it is often a Taurean's strongest area. Perhaps that is why this sign is known for being home to some of the most famous singers of all time, from James Brown to Ella Fitzgerald and Adele. Even if a Taurean does not enjoy singing, it may be beneficial to take extra care of this area by always wearing a scarf in the colder months, and avoiding drinking too much alcohol that could aggravate the throat.

Bulls are strong with a stocky build, and Taureans often find success in weightlifting or gymnastics. However, Earth is the element that guides Taurus and so physical exercise is likely to be enjoyed more so in Mother Nature than it is in the confines of a manmade gym.

Walking is a wonderful form of regular and gentle exercise that Taureans can enjoy at an adjustable speed that is comfortable for them. Not only will walking or running outdoors help with maintaining a level of physical health, it will also make sure that they stay connected to nature where they feel their calmest.

Maintaining a healthy mind is just as important as listening to what the body needs. Taureans can be stubborn and unforgiving of people that they feel have wronged them. If fixated on, this negativity can be extremely harmful for Taureans and may even manifest itself in physical pain, such as a tight neck and shoulders. By practising forgiveness and letting go of negative emotions, Taureans should find that they are much happier and healthier, and are able to refocus on what brings them joy. Exercise that centres on bringing balance to the mind as well as the body, such as yoga or t'ai chi, will help calm the aggravated Bull. Jealousy can also be another internal sore sport for any Taurean. Whilst it is a normal emotion experienced by most, Taureans can feel its sting too often in their relationships, and it may become a real cause of pain if left to fester. By questioning why these feelings of jealousy arise, Taureans can then work towards nipping those negative emotions in the bud.

Taurus

....

2020
DIARY PAGES

JANUARY

. . . .

Wednesday 1st
Happy New Year Taurus! You start the year with the
Moon in your social sector so your emotional needs
will be tied up with your groups and friends. There is
a chance you will want to drift off and indulge yourself
today, so enjoy the remainder of the festivities.

Thursday 2nd
Today your sector of adventure and exploration is
highlighted with chatty Mercury having talks with jovial
Jupiter. You may have lots of big ideas forming with
regards to your holidays for the year. This pair will help
you think big and dream big. Reach for the skies.

Friday 3rd
Your daydreams will be given more fire today as the
Moon moves into fiery Aries. You may find yourself
bringing past projects to a close and dreaming up new
ones, but remember to deal with unfinished business
first before taking on something new. You may feel
agitated and impatient today.

Saturday 4th

Mars moves into your sector of shared resources, sex, death and rebirth, today. You will want to move ahead very quickly with newly formed plans, but remember to consider those endings before planning a brand-new beginning. Do not be that bull in the china shop.

Sunday 5th

The Moon moves into your sign today making your emotional need to establish security around you very strong. This can also bring material needs too. If you are going to splash out at the January sales consider what is indulgent and what is necessary. Try to indulge your pleasures affordably.

Monday 6th

Today, and for the following week, you will feel restrictions and blockages with any future plans. Saturn is laying down the rules while Pluto keeps moving the goalposts. A very frustrating time for those adventure plans. You will feel it more personally today. Just keep breathing calmly.

Tuesday 7th

How are you doing today, Taurus? Try to look at these
frustrations as lessons and remember those endings that
need completion. Saturn is a great teacher and Pluto
strips away the unnecessary. Whilst practising your
breathing, try and take the positive lessons from these
two planets as they only want the best for you.

Wednesday 8th

Venus is checking in with you today. She is in your
career sector and is asking you to pay attention to
your obligations here. Make sure that your work is not
suffering because of these other frustrations. Spread the
Venus love in your workplace.

Thursday 9th

Breathing should be easier today as the Moon moves into
your money and security sector. Meanwhile, the Moon
and Venus are having talks today and are concerned about
the greater good. Listen carefully to what your mind is
telling you and today will bring inspiration.

Friday 10th

A full moon and lunar eclipse in your communication
and short journeys sector brings these issues up for you.
How do you communicate your needs? Mercury has
nothing to say right now, so listen to your heart instead
of your head. Today is all about where you are heading.

Saturday 11th

You will feel those restrictions again today as the Moon
sits opposite Saturn and Pluto. Today will be a good day
to sort out your wants from your needs. Can you do this?
Remember that you are in a time of shedding what no
longer serves you.

Sunday 12th

Family first today. Quality time with your loved ones
can be beneficial in re-establishing the roles you play.
Mercury joins Saturn and Pluto, so maybe your family
can supply some ideas and thoughts about what has
been holding you back. Try not to fall back into old
habits and watch your temper.

Monday 13th

A testing time which again focuses on your needs and wants. The Sun brings a little joy today so will feel lighter. A skip in your step gives you more forward motion and optimism, allowing you to see the road ahead more clearly.

Tuesday 14th

Today you could feel more sociable and want your friends around you. You will feel happy to be of service and take part in group activities. Allow yourself to dream a little and have some fun. You have more idea about plans for the future and want to share them.

Wednesday 15th

An easy day today, which continues yesterday's feelings of lightness and friendship. You have not forgotten the blocks you are facing, but today they feel less of a problem. Family and friends offer possibilities and you are happy to receive their input. Enjoy this nice space, Taurus.

Thursday 16th

Another nice day. You find a balance from within that is soothing and calming. Check in with your health today and make sure that you are getting enough rest. There is an air of excitement where lovely unexpected things could happen and surprise you.

Friday 17th

Mercury enters your career sector, kicking off a couple of weeks of work talk. Meetings, brainstorming and maybe even work trips will be on the agenda. Now is the time to put your ideas forward at work. You will have the gift of the gab if it is a promotion you are after.

Saturday 18th

Emotions run high today as the Moon enters Scorpio, your opposite sign. Sex, love and relationships will be in focus now, but be careful what you say to significant others as not everyone will be willing or able to understand deep conversations today.

Sunday 19th

Continuing from yesterday, you will be locked in passionate and secretive embraces today. These may just be in your own thoughts but you will surely uncover some little snippets of truth from deep within. Relationships will benefit from setting healthy boundaries and knowing each other's roles.

Monday 20th

You are torn between making advances in work and advances towards a lover today, Taurus. Moon, Venus and Mars are all at play, meaning that you will be emotionally pulled one way and the other. It may be best to focus on work, however, as the Sun gives added light to career goals.

Tuesday 21st

Today will see you setting your focus on work, yet there is a social element to it and you will want to be involved in a team. Try not to be the agitator in the group; innovative ideas are great but try not to be too radical today.

Wednesday 22nd

Can you possibly combine work and travel? Can you also communicate your needs at work? You have a desire to see more and do more but need to find a workable solution for this. Today is another good day for saying how you feel without being overly needy. Say it.

Thursday 23rd

As the Moon meets Jupiter today, yesterday's issues will get bigger but can be given a boost of Jupiter's joy and luck. Take advantage of this short time but do not push for too much as you may get more than you bargained for. Be respectful at all times.

Friday 24th

Today, a New Moon moves into your work sector. Do you remember at the beginning of the month you were asked to bring something to completion? If you managed to do that, then today marks the point where you can begin new projects. Passion and energy drives you.

Saturday 25th

You have a lot going on in your head today, all of which is good. You have the drive and energy to move your future plans forwards, and the mind to sort out the details. Be an ever-practical Taurus and get this down on paper.

Sunday 26th

Getting your thoughts down and wanting to act on them is where you are today. Keep that energy directed towards your goals. This will probably involve other people as you will need an outlet. Use your drive wisely, give it a purpose and a long-term role.

Monday 27th

Oh, what a lovely dreamy day today! You are so invested in your future dreams you might feel a little 'not of this world' today. Allow yourself to dream but stay grounded too. Love, idealism and romanticism feature today. Enjoy them, but do not let them derail you.

Tuesday 28th

Imagine a bull wallowing in the ocean waving to all its friends. That is you today. You are dreaming up big plans and enjoying the intoxicating waters. Do not drift too far away from the shore, and make sure that your friends are within shouting distance if you come unstuck.

Wednesday 29th

You have stepped out of the water and are drying yourself in the sun now, Taurus. That little dramatic episode is over and you have a clearer head. You are ready to march onwards and pursue those things you dreamed about. March on Taurus, you've got this.

Thursday 30th

Today you must stand and look at where you have come from and where you are going to. Keep this in mind when contemplating your next steps. Home is calling you, but so is work. Which will you choose? Take a good look before you step further into your goals.

Friday 31st

After the initial focus two days ago, you are now feeling stuck. Yesterday had you looking back and forth, and today has you thinking of the impossible tasks. Know that this will pass, but use it as a holding space in which to dig your hooves in and have a good think.

FEBRUARY

. . . .

Saturday 1st

The Moon is in your sign today dear Taurus, prepare
for your emotions to be very self-centred. As the moon
is also right on top of Uranus, sudden and unexpected
events and feelings may come up for you today. Do the
Taurus thing and stay grounded.

Sunday 2nd

Venus, the Goddess of Love, is talking with Pluto about
who is in control today. This occurs in your career sector,
maybe the soft approach can yield the better change.
With the Moon in your sign also talking to Jupiter, some
luck may come your way at work.

Monday 3rd

Money talks today as you are feeling around what you
want and how it can be acquired. Gather the facts and
do your homework before making any unnecessary
purchases. Talking to others is critical right now, as your
mind could be absent without leave for the next
few weeks.

Tuesday 4th

Dreamy Venus in your social sector is now sweet-talking Saturn in your exploration sector. Thoughts of travel and seeing new cultures come back to you. Talkative Mercury is also interrupting your thoughts, and you may be thinking of expanding this adventure into a spiritual quest or retreat.

Wednesday 5th

Your mood does not match your urge for action today. Do you want to talk about it? There is a lot of fire and air, so talk your talk and walk your walk. Watch your tongue, as you could be rather unpredictable. Think before you speak.

Thursday 6th

The Moon in your third house is once again asking you where you are going. You are feeling needy and will want to stay home with your creature comforts. Comfortable, easy conversations with loved ones are what's needed today. Listen to your soul's yearnings.

Friday 7th

Enjoy one last day of dreaming with the lovely Venus today before she turns into the Warrior Goddess. Let this be your focus and try to ignore a fleeting feeling of frustration while the Moon opposes Jupiter, Saturn and Pluto in your exploring sector. Let it go.

Saturday 8th

You'll get a power surge today as Venus drifts into Aries in full battle gear. Connect to spirit but do it with the heart of the warrior. Moon in your family sector gives you another boost to be emotionally present for others. Empathy and compassion are today's words.

Sunday 9th

The full Moon in Leo shows up for you as the king of the castle, the much-loved leader of the family or the golden child. Heartfelt emotion reigns today. See if you can hear the call of your heart and the courageous path it wants you to take.

Monday 10th

Anything creative you do today will be enhanced by the Virgo Moon. Pay attention to detail and do not cut corners. You will also feel good doing something in the service of others. Be selfless today and you will shine on your own pedestal.

Tuesday 11th

Yesterday's positivity is further enhanced today by good relations between the Moon and the big planets in Capricorn. You will still be feeling good but also less restricted in your adventure plans and your career. Keep this happy vibe going, be a Taurus and do something practical with it.

Wednesday 12th

Balance is the word for today. The Moon in lovely Libra is in your sector of duty and health. You will be feeling pulled one way and another, but the trick is to remain at the pivot point and observe. Try not to tip the balance, just watch and listen.

Thursday 13th

Those old frustrations surface today, so try to stay in yesterday's Zen. Breathe, do yoga or simply take a walk in nature. Just hold the space for yourself as this is a very short time and will soon pass. Do what Taurus does best and indulge yourself with something nice.

Friday 14th

Partners and important relationships are on your mind today, and as the Moon is in Scorpio your Valentine's Day has deep, sexy overtones. Your shadow side might show itself. You want to dive deep into the mystery of the 'other'. If you are single, your own psyche will reveal much now.

Saturday 15th

Today Mercury starts to slow down ready for another retrograde period. This is your chance to back up your devices and double-check all travel plans for the next three weeks. If there are contracts that need to be signed then try to delay them until retrograde is over.

Sunday 16th

Once again, travel is highlighted. Mars moves into your travel sector and the Moon moves into your sector that deals with sex, death, rebirth and shared finances. But remember the Mercury retrograde warning. Try to hold off making plans until it is over or they may not materialise.

Monday 17th

As Mercury is going retrograde through your social sector and a little of your career sector, bite your tongue in social groups. It's also wise to refrain from reactionary comments on social media, and best to put off being the rebel for a few weeks.

Tuesday 18th

Friendships and work colleagues get on very well today but the shared visions you may have can grow out of proportion and cause overwhelm. Everything might look like jovial dreams, but be aware of pesky Mercury as all of this may well be an illusion. Wait until the fog lifts.

Wednesday 19th

The Sun now enters your social sector while the Moon is visiting your adventure sector. Let the Sun shine on yesterday's misty dreams and look at the reality of them. A Holy Grail or a White Elephant may be revealed now, to see things for what they are, possible or impossible.

Thursday 20th

Frustrations return as the Moon passes the big planets once again. Your urge to get up and go or advance in your career is laced with responsibilities and duties. You are pulled one way and then the other and you know that what you need is change. Sit tight, this will pass.

Friday 21st

You might feel like acting on instinct today but this could have some unexpected and unpleasant results. The best thing you can do today is use that nervous energy for something physical and ground yourself. Go to the gym, for a walk or maybe do something creative today.

Saturday 22nd

The Moon shifts into your career sector and you will want to connect with others. Networking will be good for you today, but try to keep your feet on the ground as there is still that air of unpredictability and you do not want to upset colleagues.

Sunday 23rd

A New Moon in your social sector gives you the chance to look at the meaningful connections in your life. Sort through the ones that help you advance from the ones no longer serving you. Renew your connection to the greater good and listen to what your soul family is telling you.

Monday 24th

Venus the planet of love and Jupiter the planet of luck are at odds today. Your dreams and visions are in disconnect with your adventure plans. Put any travel plans to one side and let love be your guide. Allow yourself to dream and be good to yourself.

Tuesday 25th

Your energy and drive will pick up as Mars is given a short boost by the Sun. Mars will be asking you to take a good look at where you have come from and what needs to be left behind. Keep moving forward Taurus, it is the only way.

Wednesday 26th

As the Moon comes around to your dreaming sector, you might feel a little isolated and cut off today. You may feel agitated and want to end and start projects but feel too stuck to move. Thinking and speaking may feel fuzzy today so go do something practical.

Thursday 27th

More agitation today, as that group of big planets in your travel sector is being nudged by the Moon and Venus. What do you need? What do you desire? Ask these questions in relation to your duties and responsibilities. Make a list and tick some boxes.

Friday 28th

Today will see you feeling indulgent and self-centred. As we know Taurus, of all the zodiac signs you are the one who likes to spend but you also like security. Treat yourself by all means but maybe make it something that will come to be useful.

Saturday 29th

You are still feeling the urge to spend, and this is your way of having control. Your finances, your way. You may even feel like radicalising your wardrobe and changing your style to see what reactions you get. Today you are out to shock one way or another.

MARCH
....

Sunday 1st
March begins with a positive spin on all those
frustrations regarding travel and adventure. After your
spending spree where you may have spent some money
to secure some travel or booked yourself a little trip, you
will feel lighter and more positive. You can do it Taurus,
just be sensible.

Monday 2nd
The Moon is in your money sector, so maybe look at
your recent spending and review what is necessary. You
may now feel in two minds about something you bought;
something you thought was a good idea may not be so
now. All that glitters is not gold.

Tuesday 3rd
Carrying on from yesterday, you may feel like
backtracking on recent purchases. Is this good for your
bank balance? Did you make the right choice? You do
not like indecision, so think of it in terms of, 'Is it good
for me? Does it serve a purpose?'

Wednesday 4th

Your thoughts and feelings turn towards your tribe now. Having your loved ones around you means a great deal. Home comforts and friendship groups will make you feel safe and secure. Remember that Mercury is still in retrograde, so be mindful of your words with important people.

Thursday 5th

As your planetary ruler, Venus now enters your sign and gives you an added boost of confidence in matters of the heart. Venus likes the good things in life and you deserve them, however the Moon opposite Mars may make you aggressively obtain what you desire.

Friday 6th

You are still feeling the need for home comforts and to be surrounded by loved ones, but at the same time you are feeling restricted and smothered by them. Resist the urge to rebel and upset your support system. This selfish act will do you no favours in the long run.

Saturday 7th

Your inner child comes out to play today. You want to be number one in your family circle. You could be the star of the show or you could be the spoilt brat. Better to be the golden child who everyone is proud of. Let your light shine.

Sunday 8th

The planet of love wants you to be spontaneous today.
What can you do to surprise a lover? Or you may be
at the receiving end of the surprise. With the Sun also
cosying up with the planet of dreams you could be in for
a great day.

Monday 9th

A Full Moon in your creative sector highlights another
great day. You will be paying attention to detail, dotting the
is and crossing the its and making something beautiful.
You can have a fun-filled day today under the influence of
this Moon. It will also highlight any health issues.

Tuesday 10th

Hooray! The old trickster Mercury goes direct today.
Communication, travel and technology problems you
may have experienced over the last three weeks will ease
now. Venus is also asking you to assess the past and the
future, and you will be remembering good times.

Wednesday 11th

You will be putting the balance right today after the recent
Mercury retrograde. Any upsets can be corrected, any tension
can now be levelled out and any relationship problems can
be mediated with a clear head. All will be well Taurus if you
remember boundaries, yours and those of other people.

Thursday 12th

The Moon in your opposite sign of Scorpio always means that you experience deep, dark and sexy times. If you are in a relationship then this could reach another level, if you are single then this is always a good time to do your inner work.

Friday 13th

Continue with yesterday's theme. Intimacy with others or with your own psyche can reveal hidden treasure, and when the Moon is in Scorpio we can dive as deep as we like and find the gold. Today is supported by good connections to the big planets in Capricorn. Use it well.

Saturday 14th

A favourable day. The frustrations you have been feeling with regards to needs and wants, travel and responsibility are at ease today. Your get up and go has a dreamy element to it and you can accomplish much, even if it is just clear thinking.

Sunday 15th

The Moon moves into your sector of sex, death, rebirth and shared finances today. You will be thinking ahead and making more plans on adventure and travel and how this can be done with a friend or a loved one. Share the fun – and the cost!

Monday 16th

Your chatterbox mind will be dreaming away today and for the next couple of weeks. You could be gathering information on a dream holiday, a spiritual retreat or a personal vision quest. Do your research and explore everything in your mind first before committing any time or finances.

Tuesday 17th

A funny day today when ideas and plans will pop in and out of your head quite suddenly and disappear or become disregarded just as quickly. You will move between possibilities and think you can do something one moment and not the next. Think carefully.

Wednesday 18th

Today you will think about many reasons why you cannot follow through with your plans. After the initial excitement you may now feel trapped or unable to move forwards. This is just a passing Moon phase which happens every month, on these days just practise breathing and lie low.

Thursday 19th

This is a day to tie up loose ends and bring long-standing projects to completion. Spring is just around the corner and you need to think about where you are going to plant your new seeds. Taurus the practical builder has a mini empire to start building.

Friday 20th

Happy Spring Equinox! This is a time of balance and only you can decide which way to go. Are you going to keep the balance or tip it into something new? Hold this day in contemplation and consider which plans are really worth that Taurus hard work and muscle.

Saturday 21st

Emotions and mind meet today and you may feel yourself having a heart-versus-head battle. Take the pressure off and indulge your dreams. Maybe make a vision board or write your ideas down. Better out than in, it is said, and you may be able to see what was hidden.

Sunday 22nd

Today you will have some brain chatter going on and you may hear things that seem to drag you in a certain direction. Saturn the great teacher now moves into your career sector for about two and a half years and needs discipline. What can you learn for the greater good?

Monday 23rd

Mars the warrior meets Pluto the transformer today in your travel sector. You will have more energy to deal with what needs to change. Maybe some plans need to be scrapped or transformed into something better. A few tweaks to your plans might be a good idea.

Tuesday 24th

A New Moon in your dreams sector helps today with all of the ideas you have been having about retreat. Maybe a short-term retreat or just time spent alone will help you think clearly. You want to go for it but feel stuck in the mud.

Wednesday 25th

Another day for Taurus to sit, plod or sleep on it. Charging in like a bull is not going to help. You still feel fired up with plans but you need to work out which are just air castles and which can you actually build into something solid.

Thursday 26th

This could be quite an explosive day if you react rather than sit and think. The Moon in your sign makes you quite self-centred and this can have negative effects. Use that self-indulgence to do something nice for yourself!

Friday 27th

You need to be a caged bull today for your own safety. Continue with self-care, tuck yourself away with nice things around you and keep that snorting stubborn bull under control. Letting yourself loose today may not be a good thing for those around you.

Saturday 28th

Venus, your ruler and the Goddess of Love, is talking to Jupiter, the Santa Claus of the sky who is in your sign. This can only mean good things for you. What do you wish for? What are your deepest desires? Ask Jupiter and you could be surprised.

Sunday 29th

Expressing your needs and asking for what you desire could bring you some favourable results. Sometimes two heads are better than one, so talk it over with someone. You like to have nice possessions, so today give thanks for what you have.

Monday 3oth

Communications that have been difficult can become clearer today. They can also become more direct and forceful. Mars has moved into your career sector and if this is something that you want, the next few weeks are favourable for advancement in this area. Be direct but remain open.

Tuesday 31st

Short trips away or visits to the family home might be an option today. If you have your own family, time spent together today will be good for the soul. Mars is meeting Saturn the teacher today for his next instructions on his mission in your career sector.

APRIL

....

Wednesday 1st

Today is another nice day to discuss dreams, visions and possible getaways with family and friends. Those nearest to you will be able to keep you grounded so that you do not drift off into the realms of illusion. Listen to solid advice and other people's experiences.

Thursday 2nd

Still on the home front, your needs can enable some inner child play today. Be creative in whatever activity you do. Be playful too, but do not be tempted to act up or be the playground bully. Old childhood patterns of shining or hiding might surface today, recognise them for what they are.

Friday 3rd

Venus, your planetary ruler, leaves your sign today and enters your money and possessions sector. That is still okay for you as Venus loves these things too. She will give you a boost over the next couple of weeks in these areas, so remember to give thanks for the gifts.

Saturday 4th

Today Venus talks to Saturn and sweet-talks him into going easy on you. Rules may be relaxed and boundaries opened a little. Meanwhile, communication about ideas and dreams continues very strongly today. Be mindful that illusions could surface.

Sunday 5th

Some sorting for you today. You will feel more emotionally secure if you have a little declutter. This could be in the office, your home or your life. Jupiter and Pluto meet today and are asking to look at the big picture and clean it up.

Monday 6th

Are you still decluttering? What needs to be filed, stored or thrown away? Pluto wants you to transform something old into something new. What can be reduced, recycled or reused in your life? Jupiter is making this into a huge task but is happy to help.

Tuesday 7th

Something unexpected might come up for you. Uranus in your sign is at odds with Mars who wants to move forwards. Road blocks, delays or miscommunication could occur, but try to keep a level head or your health might suffer. Hot-headed bulls make more mistakes than calm cows.

Wednesday 8th

Today you have a Full Moon in your health and duty sector. When was the last time you checked in with your health? What is it that you might be doing in the 9-5 that you can drop and replace with some 'me' time? Mundane routine is highlighted for you today too.

Thursday 9th

Relationship trouble might surface as the Moon moves into your 'other' sector and makes uncomfortable positions with Mars, the God of War, and Uranus, the God of Disruption. You might want to uncover something that has been creeping around in the dark, but will it do you any good?

Friday 10th

Try not to get emotionally attached to things that are out of your control. If you decluttered a few days ago, you will remember how possessions hold certain memories and are hard to dispose of. Check where your attachments are and if they seem healthy or not.

Saturday 11th

Mercury comes back like an enthusiastic child today. Plans and new ideas enter your head and will not leave you alone. It is hard to concentrate on your daily life and you feel like drifting off into fantasy and fighting dragons.

Sunday 12th

You can feel a little more grounded, dig your hooves in and listen carefully while Mercury communicates his ideas to Saturn the Teacher. Saturn in your work sector needs you to think carefully about the radical plans in your head. How will they benefit the group and not just you?

Monday 13th

You are yearning to get away. Despite the advice of Saturn you still want to go before doing all your research. Today is best spent watching National Geographic videos to scratch that itch. A costume drama or two can help transport you into your faraway lands.

Tuesday 14th

You are up and down with emotions and frustrations. This is a difficult time in the sky for all signs with so many big planets occupying the same space. Let the Moon pass and the mood will get better.

Wednesday 15th

Does everything look bigger today? This can go either way and make bigger problems or bigger opportunities. The same frustrations are hanging around and obstacles seem too big to surmount right now. Take some downtime Taurus, there are no red flags and no green lights.

Thursday 16th

Frustrations ease today as you get a soothing effect between lovely Venus and the Moon. Your career sector and your money sector could get a boost or a short reprieve. Check bank balances, you could possibly treat yourself today with a little luxury or reward for hard work.

Friday 17th

A dreamy Moon today sees you drift around your social groups dishing out the good vibes and spreading the love. You are such a social butterfly and ray of sunshine that people will see only the lighter side of you.

Saturday 18th

Talk is productive and sweet today. It could even be laced with desire and communicated directly. Tell those closest to you how you are feeling; you may be surprised with how easy communications are today. A word of warning though, be discerning so that you do not get sucked into anything false.

Sunday 19th

Mercury is talking nicely to Mars today. That trickster is either stirring up trouble or playing the matchmaker. Beware of third parties today. If you are lucky, caring connections could be on the cards.

Monday 20th

The Sun in your sign is showing you the way forwards. You are torn between doing things for yourself and doing things for family. Your own needs will pull you in and the needs of others will pull you out. Try to find a balance and everyone will benefit.

Tuesday 21st

That tension from yesterday has now turned into a Mars and Venus struggle. What you want and how you go about getting it is where your emotional mind is at today. It is a good struggle but which craving will you satisfy? Aim for compromise.

Wednesday 22nd

As the Moon edges its way into your sign, you can feel the tension from yesterday surfacing again and you want what you want. Taurus usually gets what they ask for but try not to be a spoilt child about this. All good things come to those who wait.

Thursday 23rd

A New Moon in the early days of Taurus is like a kick-start. Projects you have pondered since the beginning of the year get some real grounding now and more potential. You are beginning to see more realistic possibilities and can plant seeds in fertile soil.

Friday 24th

Just do some gardening. You are the green fingers of the zodiac, so have a good look at yesterday's seeds and read the packets. What conditions do they need to grow? When might you see results? Will they be short or long term?

Saturday 25th

Money issues might come up as the Moon moves into your money and possessions sector. You may need to talk to someone about investing and this could be a difficult conversation. Results are on your mind and you think the best way to achieve them is to save or spend.

Sunday 26th

Pluto, the planet of power and control, goes retrograde today so for the next few months you will need to review issues on these themes where they concern both your travel plans and your career. There may also be some pleasant surprises concerning yourself.

Monday 27th

Your mood turns towards family and making short trips. Check in with loved ones. Mercury is also entering your sign, which could make you think, talk and focus solely on yourself for a few weeks. Where do you feel grounded and at home? Reflect on what makes you feel secure.

Tuesday 28th

Today you will find yourself pondering the big questions of who you are and what you are here for. Your mind reaches into the future and you have a day of self-reflection. Think about what behaviours no longer serve you, and what can you leave behind in order to progress.

Wednesday 29th

You continue to review your life and will see some light shining on areas of where you may have been controlled by others or just not in control of issues at work and also your freedom. Just have a think Taurus, now is not the time to act.

Thursday 30th

After the last few days of contemplation, you feel your inner child coming out today. That child may see issues from childhood more clearly now. Today is a good day to heal some of those childhood wounds and remember the joy and freedom that children have naturally.

MAY
....

Friday 1st
Spontaneous and rash actions and thoughts might
arise today. This might be a good thing or a bad thing.
Remember the old saying to think before you act and to
think before you speak. The energy today is about the
unexpected so you would be wise to sit tight.

Saturday 2nd
Check in with your health. Look at what is draining
your energy or how you give too much of yourself. Being
there for others is a commendable trait but make sure
you have someone there for you. Learn to take time out
and recharge.

Sunday 3rd
Stay with the health checks today as the Moon makes nice
connections to planets in Earth signs. Get grounded, go
for a walk in nature or do some yoga or meditation. Your
monkey mind will benefit from doing something physical
or focused so turn your attention to yourself.

Monday 4th

Monkey mind will either have nothing to say today or will not be clear with communication. Having checked in with your health you now want to find a happy medium between work and play. Schedule some 'me' time.

Tuesday 5th

Following on from yesterday, you might feel that you need to make some lists and timetables for yourself. Have you taken on too much? You will feel the urge to connect with the wider world but knowing you need time to yourself pulls you back. How can you remedy this?

Wednesday 6th

Further to your planning, you now see the need to also schedule in time for love. You may often be very self-centred but now your mood turns towards intimate relationships. Deep, dark and mysterious both excites and frightens you, and it won't hurt to explore.

Thursday 7th

A full Moon in your opposite sign of Scorpio can
see you enjoying some secret times with a partner.
It can also make you run and hide. What do you see
highlighted in the 'other' that attracts or repels you?
Have you thought of this as a reflection of yourself?

Friday 8th

You want to get away from it all. Your sense of adventure
kicks in and instead of looking forwards, you look
backwards at where you have already been in your life.
Time for something new, perhaps? Get out the atlas and
see where you are drawn to.

Saturday 9th

You are itching for change, and it would do you good to
talk about it. Pluto, the planet of change, is retrograde
for quite some time, so try to look at ways you can
control some small changes in your life without making
them into big dramas.

Sunday 10th

You will be feeling good about yesterday's thoughts and will have some helpful conversations or gather some new useful information today. Mercury talks to the lucky planet Jupiter on your behalf, and does a little research on the possibilities of change regarding travel and work. Listen carefully to what Jupiter says.

Monday 11th

Another big planetary retrograde today. Saturn has just dipped his toe into your career sector and is now going to reverse into your travel sector. Saturn is known as the Lord of Karma so please be careful what you do regarding travel choices until the end of September as they may have a karmic lesson for you.

Tuesday 12th

Mercury now shifts into your sector concerning money and possessions. You like money, nice things and indulgent experiences so now is the time to check your bank balance if you want these things. Splashing the cash with friends will be on your mind.

Wednesday 13th

Venus now also joins the retrograde planets. She is doing this in your money sector and she will come up against Mercury in the same sector. Any pleasure purchases bought now will be a waste of your money. This is your ruling planet so take heed.

Thursday 14th

Mars in your social sector might feel like walking through mud instead of charging on with your ambitions. Put this together with Venus retrograde and your social life could be a little strained or non-existent for a couple of weeks. Save that money and look after number one.

Friday 15th

Jupiter is going retrograde in your travel sector. Again, you will need to review any plans made in this area for the next few months. Your mood will be dreamy and sociable and on the whole you will be feeling positive, but check that you are doing the right thing.

Saturday 16th

You might feel a bit down, as if none of your plans, wishes and dreams are happening for you. This is a short transit by the Moon at odds with Venus who is retrograde. As the Moon moves quickly, so will this mood so stick at it.

Sunday 17th

New seeds of ideas begin to form in your mind. What once looked like a good idea may now be scrapped for something else. Look at all the pros and cons but do not act yet, just keep those old ideas on the back-burner.

Monday 18th

Today and tomorrow you will start to feel a little better about matters of the heart. What you want, love and desire seems more accessible. Talking about love issues will help you get a better perspective. Heartfelt communications are possible now.

Tuesday 19th

The same mood as yesterday fills you. You will want to talk with your nearest and dearest about what is on your mind and in your heart. You may feel like you are not getting what you deserve so take time out to count your blessings today.

Wednesday 20th

Today is a 'me' day for you. The moon makes its monthly visit to your sign and you will be centred on getting your needs met. There is nothing wrong with a bit of self-care but you have a habit of overindulging. Do also watch the pennies.

Thursday 21st

The Sun has just moved into your money house so you may get a financial boost this month. On the other hand you may just spend, spend and spend. With a lot of planets in retrograde, you would be wise to be careful with money.

Friday 22nd

A New Moon in your money house gives you a brand-new start with your finances and your belongings. Maybe you want to revamp your home or just invest some cash somewhere. You like pretty things but you also like security, so choose wisely.

Saturday 23rd

Your energy, drive and mood are not in sync today. You want to be with friendship groups, be present on social media but you just don't feel it today. Wait until this mood passes or you may feel drained by people. Wave your flag another day.

Sunday 24th

Show your face today, but do not commit to anything you will regret later on. The mood of the general public is to get together and march on but this is not the time to act. Go with the flow whilst keeping a respectful distance for now.

Monday 25th

Home is where the heart is, and that is where you would be better spending time today. You will want to think about your role in the family and how it affects the entire tribe. Feeling nurtured and comfortable is important for a Taurus who likes home comforts.

Tuesday 26th

Your mind will wander back to any future travel plans today and you will think about what is actually possible and what is just a dream. You will feel antagonistic towards structures beyond your control but do think why this is so. Control the small things.

Wednesday 27th

Today may put you in a very demanding mood. Resist the urge for tantrums as they will not do you any good. Instead be the delightful Golden Child and people will be more than willing to play with you.

Thursday 28th

Mercury moves into the sector of your chart that deals with short journeys and gathering data. Trips back and forth to see and speak with family could be possible, and may even open up some travel ideas for you. It is always worth listening to others' experience for your own research.

Friday 29th

Another day to check in with your health. Pay attention to all the details of your 9-5 and look at what is absolutely necessary to keep in your routine. In what ways do you serve your community? Today you may want to think about how you make a difference.

Saturday 30th

Continuing from yesterday, is there a part of you that feels empty? If so, think about ways to replenish what is missing. Perhaps you are drained or have been spending time focused on others. Be especially mindful as to how it is affecting your health.

Sunday 31st

Trying to balance your needs and everyone else's can be a daunting task sometimes. Yet you are the most dedicated and determined sign of the Zodiac and will find a way. Remember to do this with compassion and not begrudgingly as this will only make the balance harder to achieve.

JUNE
....

Monday 1st
This can be a frustrating day when nothing seems to be moving or progressing in the way you would like. Take your mind off your own problems and look to where you can help someone else. There is a certain satisfaction to be gained from helping others.

Tuesday 2nd
If you are planning on some special time with a lover please be aware that Venus and Mars are not in a position to play nicely together. The Moon in Scorpio wants to uncover secrets, and dive into those deep and dark places that Scorpio prefers to keep hidden.

Wednesday 3rd
Emotions might explode into something catastrophic today. This could be inside your head where you are making something bigger than it actually is. Family arguments can be smoothed over with some kind words, but be careful not to rebel for the sake of it. Keep your cool.

Thursday 4th

You may feel unseen and unheard today, so use that space to lie low and think up your next move. Action-orientated Mars in your social sector is getting some extra heat from the Sun, meaning things could start loosening up and moving again. That urge to get away returns.

Friday 5th

A Full Moon in your sector of sex, death and rebirth highlights what needs to be disposed of so that something else can use that space. This is a good day to shake things up a bit without being ruthless. Re-use, recycle and find the gold in the old.

Saturday 6th

A difficult time as the Moon enters the sector of your chart dealing with travel, the urge to explore new cultures and careers. Tension will build for the next few days so maybe continue with yesterday's decluttering and allow yourself to be surprised with what space you have cleared.

Sunday 7th

A good day for releasing more tension by socialising a little. Energy is still low so keep it light-hearted. The tension generated by the retrograde planets in Capricorn is still there, but networking with friends and general, all-round friendliness can help ease some of that.

Monday 8th

As the Moon crosses Pluto the Jupiter tension reaches an all-time high. You could be blowing steam, kicking your heels or stubbornly refusing to move. This will pass as quickly as the Moon changes so this is another good day to get in touch with your body and nature.

Tuesday 9th

Your attention is focused on the work place. A little bit of structure and routine will do you good and make you feel human again. There is a feeling of sociability and friendliness around you, which brings you back down to earth. Feel the love.

Wednesday 10th

Your ego is at odds with your dreams today. You could feel like things are dissolving around you, but these things are superficial and are on the ego level. They may even make way for some of the real you to start showing up.

Thursday 11th

Sharing dreams with friends might help you today but you may also feel like retreating into your own little world. The danger of this is that you might feel the need to self-medicate with alcohol, cake or too much TV, so it is best to use this time with friends.

Friday 12th

Once again, you will be feeling self-indulgent and sorry for yourself. You want to be alone or are resentful that you have to be. Try to get out and socialise, even if it is video messaging. You don't have to be alone today Taurus, you are loved.

Saturday 13th

Another day where wallowing under the duvet seems the better option. Binge-watching a TV show or films by yourself may seem tempting, but being within friendship groups or involved in lively debates would be good for your soul. Make an effort and be present.

Sunday 14th

As the Moon passes into Aries, you feel more optimistic. It is okay to be alone now because your mind and heart are occupied with projects that need your attention and that you are happy to engage in. New things will also come into your head, keep them in mind.

Monday 15th

There is a lot of chatter in your head. You have the beginnings of new ideas and the itch to get on with them, but you need to get these out of your head and be the ever-practical Taurus and get them down on paper.

Tuesday 16th

Easy connections between the Sun and Moon, as well as the Moon entering your own sign, make today very positive and uplifting. A word of warning; finish some projects before starting new ones as Mercury is about to go retrograde and will make things difficult for you.

Wednesday 17th

Loose ends in your career and travel plans need to be attended to before Saturn retreats into your sector of shared finances, sex, death and rebirth. Finish these up and take care to make sure that all involved are informed and that you are all on the same page.

Thursday 18th

Mercury retrograde warning. What has been going on for you in the last few weeks regarding short trips, siblings or communication? Be mindful of these issues until mid-July and remember the usual thing to do is back off, double check and try not to sign any contracts during this time.

Friday 19th

Today is one of those days where it is suddenly glaringly obvious what path you need to follow. The Sun crosses a point in the sky that beckons us onwards to our futures. Mars the destroyer talks to Pluto the transformer and between them they tear down the old.

Saturday 20th

Mars, now in the final section of your social sector, is talking to retrograde Jupiter in your travel sector. Are you thinking of travelling with a group of friends? Mars wants to let go of some unrealistic ideas you have been having and only focus on what is achievable.

Sunday 21st

There is a big Solar Eclipse on the New Moon in Cancer today, and it is right on the Summer Solstice. The day of longest light will be overshadowed briefly, so what does that mean for you? You must look at what you have before the urge to acquire more.

Monday 22nd

A nurturing Moon asks that you look at home, family and mother issues. If your loved ones are far away, a phone call or message could make you and the family you contact feel good. You may also want to look at your own style of nurturing.

Tuesday 23rd

It is Inner Child time again, Taurus. Try and have fun, maybe meet with some old school friends or visit places you enjoyed as a child. Whenever the inner child comes out to play, remember to look out for old patterns that no longer serve.

Wednesday 24th

Neptune the planet of dreams and illusions went retrograde yesterday in your social sector. At this time you could be lulled into a false sense of security or a dream that is not all that it seems. Use your Taurus energy and stay practical and grounded.

Thursday 25th

Venus, your planetary ruler, goes direct today so any affairs of the heart that you have experienced over the last forty days will now either become clearer or will have dissolved into the past. You will now see the bigger picture behind any make-ups or break-ups that have occurred.

Friday 26th

There is an itchy energy today because Mars is taking a look at where he has been and where he is going, and is being pulled both ways. For you, that means short-distance travel and familiarity versus long-distance travel and everything foreign. Look both ways, Taurus.

Saturday 27th

A critical point for Mars in your social sector. There may be people or groups in your life that you leave behind now before you charge ahead. A Libra Moon will see that you do it fairly and that it does not negatively impact on your daily life.

Sunday 28th

Mars is now free in your dreaming sector. Do you have a vision quest that his energy can help you with? Do you have thoughts about being the spiritual warrior? Do you have a sacred purpose that you would like to follow up on? Let Mars be your guide for this.

Monday 29th

You feel the restrictions of all those retrograde planets in Capricorn today. Remember that with Mars in your dreaming sector, those travel plans you have had this year could be pointing towards something more like a personal inner travel. You do not need to go far to find yourself.

Tuesday 3oth

You need to get your significant other on-board with
some self-discovery. This will help you explore one
another's inner psyches before understanding your own.
Allow the Scorpio Moon to guide you on a journey of
discovery that will have deep meaning for you.

JULY

....

Wednesday 1st

Mercury has nothing to say again today. Thinking and
communicating ideas could feel muddled, blocked or
foggy. As he is in your social sector, beware of going with
the flow or falling in with the masses. You need your own
voice but cannot find it today. Make no commitments.

Thursday 2nd

Saturn has reversed back into your travel sector. What
needs to be tweaked regarding travel plans? Saturn as
the teacher is asking you to tick all the boxes and ensure
that this is right for you. Your mood reaches out and
wants to know what it is all about today.

Friday 3rd

You are in a searching mood today, you think deeply
about issues of power and control, and how you can
change things for the better. You feel unsettled and have
a need to explore things that are foreign or strange.
Other cultures and other religions interest you now.

Saturday 4th

Your mood turns towards work. You still feel unsettled and will maybe start looking at how you can change your career and combine that with your thirst for adventure. Foreign correspondence in the work place could provide some open avenues for you to scratch this itch.

Sunday 5th

A Full Moon and lunar eclipse in your travel sector could reveal some deep emotions connected with work and travel. You may feel hard done by or blocked at every turn. Look inside and check to see if those blocks aren't made by you. Are you self-sabotaging, Taurus?

Monday 6th

Today your mood is lighter and more sociable. You may feel rebellious and want to upset the status quo at work, or you may feel that others around you have the answers you are seeking. The Moon and Venus help make this a sweet, smooth day so do not start a revolution!

Tuesday 7th

Yesterday's mood continues as your ruler Venus is in your money sector. Today could be a good day to treat yourself without breaking the bank. Time spent with work colleagues will be light-hearted and chatty. Maybe an after-work dinner with a group would be just the thing.

Wednesday 8th

Mars (actions) and Mercury (words) are at odds today, plus Mercury is still in retrograde. Mind your words, as this combination makes for a very volatile day for hot-headed bulls. Also, be very careful on the roads as accidents could happen.

Thursday 9th

A dreamy, idealistic Moon in your social sector has now moved away from those nice talks with Venus. You could be a sulking bull, maybe licking your wounds from something that happened yesterday. You will refuse to move from your point of view and will only please yourself.

Friday 10th

You are in a self-destruct or self-soothe mood, and it is your choice which way to go. Self-soothing would be a better option as you need to keep a low profile. What have you done that has caused you, or someone important to you, harm? Think on it.

Saturday 11th

Today you will feel the stirrings of something new deep inside. You will look at your connection to your spirituality and wonder how you can do something to honour that. Again the spiritual warrior rises inside you and surprises you. You want to do something practical about it.

Sunday 12th

Mercury retrograde is over and so now you can go and apologise to people you may have argued with and try to put things right. Look back at the last three weeks at things that did not go to plan as you now have a chance to correct them.

Monday 13th

Your mood turns inwards to your own needs and you want everyone to know it. Put yourself in the public eye and see what is reflected back at you. This is a mirror of your own psyche – it comes from you and not from those outside of you.

Tuesday 14th

The Sun is now shining right at Jupiter in your travel sector and is showing you the bigger picture. This could be another viewpoint on what you perceive as restrictions, but which is actually a stroke of luck that you may have overlooked. Some emotional outbursts could surprise you today.

Wednesday 15th

Today the Sun is shining its light on Pluto, also in your travel sector. It will make you see where you have been in control or not. This could be a power struggle that you now clearly see for what it is. Take a step back and assess your role in this.

Thursday 16th

A favourable day for money and possessions where
you will desire something new, but are mindful of your
needs and wants. Money spent on travel plans will be
a worthy investment, and will make you feel good even
without tangible results.

Friday 17th

The Moon meets Venus again in your money sector,
which enhances the good feeling from yesterday.
Even though you have invested some funds or bought
something new for a trip you cannot see or use yet, you
know it is a spend in the right direction.

Saturday 18th

Family time today, whether that be emails, phone calls
or messages to your loved ones. Check in with everyone
and talk about your future plans. A little excitement and
encouragement today from family members will go a long
way to satisfy your urge to move forwards in your life.

Sunday 19th

You will have a lot of mind chatter today, Taurus. Thoughts will come quickly and will go again just as quickly. You have many things to think about. You can express your needs easily and will receive the same easy expression back from others. A good day for brainstorming with friends.

Monday 20th

A New Moon in your family sector asks you to consider the needs of the whole versus the needs of yourself. Is there someone with whom you need to reconnect? You will be thinking about what home means to you and how you can make improvements.

Tuesday 21st

Children could play a role today. Again your Inner Child comes out to play. When the Moon travels through this sector of your chart you could be thrown back to childhood habits and behaviours. Children can teach you to have fun and be creative.

Wednesday 22nd

The Sun moves into your home and family sector today and will be there for the next month. Now is a good time to have a good look at your role in the family. Are you the golden child or the black sheep? Stand in your own individual light.

Thursday 23rd

You might surprise yourself today, Taurus. You could be in a creative mood and express yourself with words, maybe poetry. You will not know where this sudden inspiration has come from. You will be happy with mundane life and could even be whistling while you work

Friday 24th

Today could be a bit of a disappointment after yesterday's upbeat mood. Dreams, memories and visions seem to dissolve away and you cannot get a grip on the creativity you had. Things could float around in your head and heart but not touch ground for you today.

Saturday 25th

Today you will manage to find a balance with yesterday's drifting around. You can have one foot on the ground and one foot in the ocean of your dreams. You will also be figuring a special person into your vision for future plans. How can you be of service?

Sunday 26th

Try to keep that balance steady today. Mind chatter will try to sway the tipping point or another person's words could outweigh your own. Today is a day where head versus heart needs to rest. This is a brief feeling and will pass so it is best not to upset the balance for now.

Monday 27th

Lovers, or potential lovers, could be the reason for a lot of upset. There are many difficult positions with the planets today, and as the Moon moves into your 'other' sector there could be arguments. Your needs will be completely at odds with that special other.

Tuesday 28th

Jupiter lends a hand today and you feel less alone with your visions. You may get some luck today and smooth over disagreements with others, who could now see your side or you see theirs. Dreams seem bigger but not unattainable.

Wednesday 29th

There appears to be some settling down on the relationship front and things will be a lot smoother now. You either know that something is done and dusted or it has all been forgiven and forgotten. The Moon in your sex, death and rebirth sector highlights endings and beginnings.

Thursday 3oth

Mercury in your sector of short trips is talking to Jupiter
in your travel sector. He is also talking to Neptune who
rules dreams so once again, your dreams, visions and
travel is a major focus for you. Jupiter and Neptune are
both retrograde though so take note but do not act.

Friday 31st

The Moon enters your travel sector and you yearn to
get these plans off the ground. It is okay to do this, but
it is important that you wait until things are clearer
before acting on this impulse. Watching a good travel
documentary might soothe you.

AUGUST
. . . .

Saturday 1st

Mercury, in your sector of short journeys and communication, is having a confrontation with Pluto, the Lord of the Underworld, today. Mercury the Messenger is either struggling to hear or just not listening to his next assignment of power and change. Listen but wait before acting today, Taurus.

Sunday 2nd

Being yourself can be difficult today as you feel the need to shock or surprise people. Uranus in your sign wants to uproot, disturb and unsettle but your soul essence, the Sun, is making it seem like nobody cares and wants you to toe the line today.

Monday 3rd

A Full Moon in your career sector today can reveal more than you bargained for. That little rebel inside you wants to get out and start a revolution but someone might beat you to it. Rules and regulations come under scrutiny today, a breakthrough could happen.

Tuesday 4th

There is still an urge for action in you, but it could be all in your head and in the planning stages. Your thoughts could be rebellious, even if your actions say otherwise. Keep that spiritual warrior in mind and think how you could lead for the greater good.

Wednesday 5th

A Pisces moon drifts into your friendship sector while Mercury entering your family sector has you reminiscing about the good old days. Family and friends gather together now, and some easy times can be had by all. Idealism, fond memories and long-lost dreams are remembered.

Thursday 6th

Your ruler Venus asks you to think about your desires and your materialism. You have many things on your wish list and could be in a spending mood. Luxuries attract you and propel you forward. A satisfying mood of getting what you want prevails, but is it really worth it?

Friday 7th

After yesterday's Venus mood, she now enters your sector of communication. She has a motherly feel, and you may get that little voice in your head which sounds like your own mother asking if what you have recently bought is really necessary. Mother knows best, Taurus.

Saturday 8th

Until the 21st, Mercury will be flying though your family sector and will want to get as much said as possible in this time. Today you feel positive about expressing yourself in the safety of your family, and your role within the unit is respected and honoured now.

Sunday 9th

There is tension today as your need to explore and get away comes back to you. Rest assured that this is a passing phase and whilst not much can be done about it, tension is a good thing as it is able to hold two opposing forces with ease.

Monday 10th

The Moon enters your sign and makes you self-centred. Outbursts and sudden, out-of-character speeches or acts may make the day volatile. It is best to use that self-centred feeling and turn it into self-care or otherwise just have a little 'me' time.

Tuesday 11th

Today you need to get things off your chest. Let's talk about you, Taurus. What is it you want? What will make you feel good? What do you need to feel safe and secure? Saying what is in your mind and heart will get it out there for you to deal with.

Wednesday 12th

Planning and gathering data or research will be a
good activity for you. Make short trips, communicate
with others and get to know the lay of the land for any
projects you may have. You may feel conflicted so be
sure to talk with others.

Thursday 13th

The two rulers of your opposite sign of Scorpio are
having tactic talks today. The warrior will not budge
and the transformer says that something has to
change. This will affect you with any new plans that
you have conceived. You may need to discard some in
order to move on.

Friday 14th

Change is necessary for growth, Taurus. Your mind wants
to wander away to the spiritual world with great new
ideas. Maybe you are planning a retreat. You will need to
fix these ideas in reality before acting on them. Do not
drift too far away.

Saturday 15th

The Moon meets Venus today in your short trips and communications sector. There is lovely, easy energy for you to go out and get what you want and need. These are opposite all those restrictions in your travel sector and will take some of the pressure off there too.

Sunday 16th

Uranus goes retrograde today in your sign. He is such a slow mover that you probably will not notice it, but you may find that life's surprises do not come your way for a while. Things may seem to solidify or get stuck.

Monday 17th

There's easy family energy today as the Moon makes its monthly visit to your home and family sector. Remember that for you this could mean being the golden child or the sulky toddler. Just be the entertainer and allow yourself to play and have fun. Be creative too.

Tuesday 18th

A new Moon in your home sector will look at how you shine out and what your sacred essence looks like. How do you lead others? How are you the star in your own show? Do look at the negative side and consider any narcissistic traits that you may have.

Wednesday 19th

Please check in with your health, Taurus. Are you feeling burnt out? Look at where your energy is going and if your activities nourish you or drain you. Helping others is a great virtue, but only if you are filling your cup first. Look out for psychic vampires.

Thursday 20th

A drifty, dreamy kind of day where you may be torn between switching off and doing your own thing away from the group or completely immersing yourself in social activities. Is there something you are hiding? Are you self-avoiding in order not to deal with something painful?

Friday 21st

Today is another day in which you need to find some sort of balance. This could very well be about your energy again. It could also be about how you are selfish or self-less. Are you a giver or a taker? Look at these issues today and contemplate them.

Saturday 22nd

The Sun now moves into your creativity and leisure sector. You may now start thinking about something fun you would like to do, perhaps a new hobby or course just for your own pleasure. You might find something that you can dedicate yourself to and enjoy very much.

Sunday 23rd

Your significant other, or the other half of yourself, needs attention. It's time for you to be selfless and attend to the needs of another person. This could also mean that you benefit as this time could be intimate and satisfying. Delicious treats should be on today's menu.

Monday 24th

Your energy and drive could be halted today with a big, red stop sign. Saturn is putting the brakes on Mars today, but luckily this is all in your head. Ideas and thought patterns will come under scrutiny and may be binned all together. You can feel disappointed and dejected today.

Tuesday 25th

Mercury whispers to Uranus that he needs to move a little, shake a little and oil his joints but he is not listening. Some gentle exercise might relieve the stuckness you feel. The two favourable planets, Venus and Jupiter, are in conflict but there are only pleasant times on trips for you today.

Wednesday 26th

Keep moving forwards with a little spring in your step, Taurus. Enjoy this easy energy while you can. Getting out and about, walking, driving or just visiting new places will do you some good, make you feel more positive and give you a healthy glow.

Thursday 27th

Today you will be thinking about what you want, and wondering about how you can get it. There is no limit to your fantasies, and you can make plans to go for what it is you are lusting after. Plans may be all they are today.

Friday 28th

Yesterday's fantasies continue and you feel a little agitation because you want to act on them. You must assess similar situations and desires in the past and look at what the outcome was back then. Is there a lesson you can learn from those times?

Saturday 29th

Now you feel stuck and hindered in your progress. The fantasies in your head are still there, but you feel the urge to build on them whilst having a complete understanding of why you cannot. This may make you a sulky bull. Come back down to earth and be your practical self.

Sunday 30th

Issues of power and control surface today, Taurus. This can be about the opposite sex and mainly about important partnerships. Do not rule out work partnerships too. Equality is something that you will be thinking of and you will be waving the revolutionary's flag today.

Monday 31st

Driven by your mood for fairness at work, your energy will be at a high level and you will be thinking up ways in which you can correct slights that may have happened to you or others. You stand up for the underdog today even if it is just in principle.

SEPTEMBER
....

Tuesday 1st
Mercury in your creative sector is thinking up things
to do and talking to Pluto about making changes. A
new project seems like a good idea now. Upcycling old
furniture or redecorating your home would be good too.
A floaty Moon enters your social sector.

Wednesday 2nd
The floaty Moon becomes full and spotlights your
dreams and visions regarding friendship groups. Rules
are softened now by Venus' influence and some nice
surprises could transpire for you. This can be quite a
magical day if you let yourself relax and receive whatever
the spirits want to offer you.

Thursday 3rd
Thoughts come easily today and communication flows
between you and those in authority. Listen and learn
as a teacher may come along and give you good solid
advice. The next few days are good for ending something
before taking on something new. You may feel like taking
up a new educational course.

Friday 4th

There could be a battle of the sexes today as Venus, your ruler, confronts her lover Mars. Mars is unlikely to win, and this will affect any radical plans you may have dreamt up. Venus wants you to stay close to home now.

Saturday 5th

The trickster Mercury has just moved into your health sector. You should be thinking about making all those appointments you have put off. You should also be thinking about how you give to others and, as Mercury talks to the Goddess of Love today, thinking about your relationships.

Sunday 6th

The Moon pays her monthly visit to your sign and these are the days in the month where you just want 'me' time. Your planetary ruler, Venus, steps into your family sector, making this a nurturing month rather than a selfish, indulgent month for you. Relax and enjoy.

Monday 7th

Nothing earth-shattering happens today as the Moon passes Uranus, which is stuck in your sign. An easy connection with Jupiter holds you in a comfortable position. You feel satisfied and have just enough of the right things around you to enjoy that Taurus life without going overboard.

Tuesday 8th

Today you will be thinking about your money situation and will feel pleased for the moment. You might feel in two minds about a major spend, but will likely err on the cautious side and be happy with that. Your security needs will thank you for that at a later date.

Wednesday 9th

Another comfortable day. The Sun and Jupiter are in good connection, and your big travel plans come back to you. The Moon and Venus make this a happy homely day. Talking about plans with loved ones can be both delightful and satisfying.

Thursday 10th

Mars the warrior is now going retrograde in your dream sector. This will be a very frustrating time for any vision quests or retreats you may have thought about. Time spent alone may not be what is right for you at the moment. On the other hand you could be forced to do just that.

Friday 11th

Dreams could be illuminated today for what they truly are. The Sun shines directly on Neptune and exposes anything that is false. Watch out for deceivers today as they can be unmasked, so you would be wise not to be one of them.

Saturday 12th

You feel irritable and have the desire to shock or unsettle people. This is not going to work, as the only person it will shock will be you. Change what you can, control what you can, but leave all else alone.

Sunday 13th

There is strange energy in the skies today. The giant Jupiter is now direct and can bring a change of fortune in your travel sector, but the Moon in your family sector is challenging that retrograde Mars in your dreams sector. Things move forwards in one way but are very stuck in another.

Monday 14th

Did you consider what you can change and control, Taurus? If you did, then today is a favourable day to do it and if you did not then today will be equally as good to think more about it. Balance and harmony is resuming, karma is coming.

Tuesday 15th

You look back into the past and wonder how you were propelled forwards to where you are now. You may be reminiscing about things that you used to enjoy very much but no longer do. Your health needs a check-up again over the next couple of days. Conserve your energy.

Wednesday 16th

Themes today are continued from yesterday, are you feeling drained and depleted? Take a look at your mundane daily tasks and other projects you have taken on and see if there is anything that no longer excites you. Let it go, give yourself some extra time.

Thursday 17th

A New Moon in your creativity and self-expression sector asks you how you are showing up in the world. Are you being authentically you or are you hiding under someone else's glory? Stand up Taurus, show us your horns, come outside and play. It will be good for your soul.

Friday 18th

Harmony and balance come up again, and for you that means taking a review of your time management. As a Taurus you are no stranger to being number one, but are you really giving yourself the time you need? Take more care of yourself before seeing to others.

Saturday 19th

Today, you will be quite touchy and irritable. The Moon in your opposite sign wants to wallow in self-pity as it has just passed a retrograde Mars in your dream sector, and is now in a stand-off with Saturn and Pluto.

Sunday 20th

There is still an edgy feeling in the air. You want to host a stampede and get things moving or raise a revolution but it is just not happening for you. Are you a rebel without a cause? Find something worth shouting about and get attention that way.

Monday 21st

How far are you willing to go? How deep are you willing to dive? Your heart is carrying you to far-off places inside and outside of you that you never knew existed. You are trying to reason all of this out but you cannot. Go with the flow.

Tuesday 22nd

Your mind is full of the past and the future. You have nice memories combined with optimistic plans. As the Sun moves into your house of duty, health and routine you are again finding a balance in your life. Try to find that point without tipping.

Wednesday 23rd

That little devil on your shoulder will give you all the reasons why you cannot follow through with your plans. You would do best by listening with an observer's ear and not reacting or responding. There may well be some nuggets of wisdom for you here.

Thursday 24th

Today is mind versus action. The mind is going to win as you will do nothing today to act on your thoughts. This is a good thing because the action part concerns Mars retrograding in your house of dreams. Stay grounded and stubborn Taurus, and you know that you can do that.

Friday 25th

Your emotional state can be a little mixed today and you can become uncertain about future travel pans and your career. This is because Jupiter, the lucky planet, is the only one that is in direct motion. All will be clear soon enough.

Saturday 26th

Today is a fairly easy-going day. Time spent with friends or even work colleagues would give you some fun. If your idea of fun is fighting for justice you can do that too. Lead the masses and stand out in the crowd today but enjoy the party when you do.

Sunday 27th

Mercury dives deep into Scorpio waters today and this is where your love life lies. If you are not already attached, now is the time to put the word out there and let someone know your feelings. Messages and emails could bring some secrets to be kept or revealed.

Monday 28th

Another sociable day. Do not drink too much as the tendency will be to drift away on your own and who knows where you may end up. Stick with friends and be safe. Float around with the crowd today and enjoy going with the flow.

Tuesday 29th

More restrictions are lifted today as Saturn goes direct. You may now be able to see that some things you wanted to do were a bad idea in the first place. On the other hand you may have already done these things and are now regretting them.

Wednesday 30th

The Moon is having talks with the planets in your travel sector and you feel more satisfied with getting things going again. However, a bad-tempered Mars in your dreaming sector is having a lesson from Saturn on how to behave around other people and what is good etiquette.

OCTOBER

. . . .

Thursday 1st
A Full Moon in your dreaming sector will show where
you hide and retreat and what dreams are possible or
just illusions. Take care, as the tendency will be to self-
medicate with something that will make you switch off.
Better to use alone time to heal and not to isolate yourself.

Friday 2nd
Venus moves into your creative sector and you could
now be redecorating your home or revamping your style.
Young children will play a part for the next couple of
weeks, and will teach you how to have fun and laughter.
Venus also wants you to learn about self-care.

Saturday 3rd
The Moon is making a lovely connection from your
sign to Venus. You will feel pleasantly indulgent without
going overboard. You may want to have a pamper session
at a spa or fill your mind, body and soul with nourishing
and beautiful things. You deserve it, Taurus.

Sunday 4th

Anything could happen as the Moon passes Uranus in your sign and sits opposite Mercury. You could say something shocking or even hurtful, so be careful with words today and remember to think before you speak. You could use this influence to be innovative and blaze a trail.

Monday 5th

Pluto goes direct today, so that means that now all of the planets moving slowly in your travel sector are on-board for more forwards motion. It has been a long time of blocks and frustrations for you, but finally you will see the road you are about to travel.

Tuesday 6th

Money and possessions will be on your mind, and that will be no surprise to you. You may be in two minds about spending, so get out of your own head and ask someone's advice. You feel positive and upbeat but vacillate between two choices.

Wednesday 7th

Another day where you should be cautious with words. There is an old saying that asks that before you speak, consider if it is true, kind and necessary. If you remember this then you cannot go wrong and will be less likely to say something shocking.

Thursday 8th

The Moon moves into the area of your chart that deals with short journeys and communication. This could be a day when you have a lot of little jobs to do or a lot of visits to make. Family is also highlighted here so small get-togethers are likely.

Friday 9th

The two rulers of your opposite sign are not in a good connection today. Pluto in your travel sector is telling Mars in your dream sector that something has to change. Mars does not like this and will stand his ground. Who will win Taurus? What needs to change?

Saturday 10th

Venus glosses over any radical behaviour you may have displayed recently. As your ruler, she can mother and nurture you or entice you to be very self-indulgent. Here she gives you motherly advice and teaches you to laugh at your outspokenness, whilst reminding you not to do it again.

Sunday 11th

The Moon in your family sector makes you want to feel like number one today but it is also making uneasy connections to Uranus and Mercury, and your need to be outrageous surfaces once again. Be warned Taurus, if you do it again it will not end well for you.

Monday 12th

Today you will be thinking about the recent past and wondering what on earth made you say or do something that did not put you in good light. You do not like to be thought of badly, so you must think of a way to put things right now.

Tuesday 13th

Aggressive actions will be exposed today. These could be yours or another's directly affecting you. This could even just be thoughts in your head. Watch your blood pressure and other health issues as you are not doing yourself any favours.

Wednesday 14th

Now you have Mercury retrograde in your sector of relationships, which means your recent reckless words and behaviour are not going to be forgiven just yet. Your negative mood will continue for a couple of weeks and you will be a raging bull. Again, watch your health.

Thursday 15th

Advice for the next couple of days is to concern yourself with your day-to-day duties, as it could help balance out your irritable mood. It is best not to expect too much from others, so keep your head down and just get on with the jobs you need to.

Friday 16th

A new Moon in your health and routine sector is urging you to find balance between work and play. Take a good look at which health routines you could change or make better, and what daily routines are just not necessary or are draining your resources.

Saturday 17th

Remember that Mercury retrograde in your relationship sector? Today the Moon passes over it and also sits opposite Uranus, who likes to upset the status quo. Today is not a good one for romance, so stay in and wash your hair.

Sunday 18th

Today you will have a lesson about boundaries. You will learn where you end and another person begins. This will most likely be your partner or the most significant person in your life. Give the other some space and remember that you are two separate people.

Monday 19th

Venus and Mars are both making connections to Jupiter in your travel sector. Venus is speaking kind words of service and duty, but Mars is making his own problems bigger by not listening to good advice. Dreams and goals are blocked today, but they are just dreams and nothing tangible yet.

Tuesday 20th

Be careful, as anything could happen. The shock
factor is still with you, so see if you can turn that
around and make it into a nice surprise for someone
special. The Moon is asking you to look at how you
can be kind to others today.

Wednesday 21st

The Moon moves into your travel sector today and your
thoughts return to far-off lands. Venus is having a nice
conversation with Uranus, the God of Change, because
she wants something from him. What is it you would
like, Taurus? Maybe just ask for it.

Thursday 22nd

The Sun enters your relationship sector so the mood
could be a little lighter in this area, although it also means
the spotlight is not on you. Can you handle that? You
want to move forwards in your travel plans again today.

Friday 23rd

Your career is in focus, so is there something you want
to speak out about? Can you do this with respect and
honesty? Your ruler, Venus, is giving you a helping hand
to say what is on your mind without causing any upset.
Venus wants to serve you well.

Saturday 24th

Venus is helping you out once more. She is talking to Saturn, the teacher, in your travel sector and learning what she can from him about how to plan your future correctly. Listen to what Saturn says as his advice, though sometimes harsh, is always the best.

Sunday 25th

Mercury has nothing to say to you. Instead, he wants you to listen with your heart. The Moon enters your social sector and is making nice connections to your feelings about the past and future. Some time spent with friends and social groups can help you hear what your heart has to say.

Monday 26th

Quite a delightful day. Your emotions can feed back to your mind and be held there without the need for action. You feel at peace and some welcome surprises could come your way. Give thanks for friendships and support groups today.

Tuesday 27th

Your mood is still light and airy with some positive vibes about your travel plans. You can now see what were just impossible dreams and what are new true possibilities. The lack of action at the moment does not matter, it is all still in the planning stage and in a much better position.

Wednesday 28th

As the Moon drifts into your dreaming sector, Mercury wants you to take another look at the balance between what you think and what you say. Venus enters the beginning of your health and routine sector and is also asking you to check the balance here.

Thursday 29th

You may feel a little irritable and want to move onwards, but have learned a valuable lesson in waiting until the big picture is clearer. Use that tension to do something good for your body. Go for a walk, a run or put energy into something nurturing.

Friday 30th

The Moon enters your own sign which, as always, can make you self-indulgent and obnoxious. Enjoy something that will benefit your health now. Take a look at what you have done before to feel good in your body or try some new type of exercise or food.

Saturday 31st

A Full Moon in your sign could mean that you will be a little unpredictable today. The Sun is shining on Uranus in your sign too, so the shock factor could return. Make sure that your behaviour does not upset anyone, particularly your significant other or someone close to you.

NOVEMBER

....

Sunday 1st

Your heart expands a little and emotions get bigger, but there is happiness here. There is a nice connection between the Moon in your sign and Jupiter in another Earth sign. You feel positive and optimistic today. The Sun shines on any factors that may disrupt and antagonise you.

Monday 2nd

The Moon moves into your money sector and makes a nice, easy connection to Saturn who will teach you something about where your money is going. A good day for finances whether that is saving or spending. You will know your limits today Taurus, good for you.

Tuesday 3rd

Sex appeal and romantic thoughts are on your side. Your energy and drive to please someone and make harmony in your love life is strong, and you will be fair and tender. You can pursue what you desire, but with compassion.

Wednesday 4th

Mercury resumes a forwards motion today and this helps smooth over any upsets you may have experienced in the retrograde period. You can begin to put things right in your love life and also your daily routines. Health will pick up again and you will feel better about yourself.

Thursday 5th

The Moon moves into your sector of short trips, siblings and communication. However, it is not in a good position to your ruler Venus, so you will need to put your needs to one side and do a little bit of running around pleasing other people.

Friday 6th

Watch your temper. Your mood does not match your energy and you will become agitated and possibly aggressive. Maybe you feel you have done too much for other people and not enough for yourself recently. Keep your cool as this will pass quickly.

Saturday 7th

Yesterday's mood continues and you will have to curb that instinct to show off, especially in front of your family. Avoid sulking or shouting, as these will not make you look very good when you genuinely want or need attention in the future. Be a model family member today.

Sunday 8th

Whilst the Sun is in Scorpio, your opposite sign, you will be looking at the shadow side of yourself. This is a golden opportunity to dig for gold deep down in your psyche, but the tendency is to stamp about and demand that you are the centre of attention. That is your shadow.

Monday 9th

Tensions are still high today as Venus, your ruler, opposes her lover, Mars. Venus wants peace and harmony in your daily routine, but Mars wants action. Resist the urge to upset the status quo, Venus knows best in this situation.

Tuesday 10th

Today you may have a last-minute chance to say what is on your mind and deep in your heart. Psychology doesn't really interest you but, if you can find someone willing to talk, you may find out something of deep value concerning how you relate to other people.

Wednesday 11th

Your travel plans come back into your mind and you notice that the yearning is still there. Work or play? Why not both? How can you do this? Can your career be combined with travel? Look at the possibilities.

Thursday 12th

The Moon in your routine and health sector sits next to Venus, and they discuss your desires and how to take care of yourself. Whilst this is happening, Jupiter and Pluto meet in your travel sector. This forebodes a change that dives so deep that life will never be the same again.

Friday 13th

Listen carefully and explore all avenues today, as that change in your travel and work sector may be just the thing you have been seeking this year. The Moon passes through your love sector and is helping you scan the bottom of your soul to bring things to the surface.

Saturday 14th

Mars, in your sector of dreams and solitude, goes direct today, which means that any plans, visions and solitary pursuits will have the green light. You will now see momentum in this area. Things are finally moving forward for you.

Sunday 15th

A New Moon in your love sector suggests that your focus is now on loving, balanced relationships. However, this New Moon is deep, dark and secretive and can transform anything it touches. Are you ready for a relationship like that? This could be disastrous or healing.

Monday 16th

Luck and love are at odds, so it is best not to push things as you will come away the loser. The Moon is still in your love sector and things could be intense, but not in a good way. Stick to the mundane activities today to err on the safe side.

Tuesday 17th

Someone will want to talk about matters that touch them deeply, but you are not willing to listen. This could also be the deepest parts of you wanting to surface. Chaos in the head and old behaviour patterns could cause some outrageous actions.

Wednesday 18th

You have the urge to keep pushing on certain issues. Hopefully, these are your own issues that need working out. If they do involve another person you should learn to be driven but compassionate. You can be motivated today but emotionally drained by it all.

Thursday 19th

The mood lifts. You will be willing to recognise restrictions and boundaries and will once again be yearning for distant lands. You want to try something new and foreign to you, and you have more respect for other kinds of people. Listen carefully and you may learn something today.

Friday 20th

The Moon enters your career sector, but it is not a favourable day and you will need to watch what you say and do. Controversial behaviour and speaking without thinking will be the flavour of the day. You want to say and do what is on your mind, but beware.

Saturday 21st

Venus enters your opposite sign of Scorpio which can bring some zest to your love life, and with the Sun entering your sector which deals with sex, death and rebirth you could be in for a very interesting time. These transits could also show your shadow side.

Sunday 22nd

The Moon in your social sector adds a dream-like quality to your love life. Is it too good to be true? You may now see yourself reflected in another person, and you must take care to recognise borders and know what is you and what is the other.

Monday 23rd

Sweet-talking your significant other or anyone who means a lot to you comes easy today. You are still in a floaty, dreamy mood and you will need to see what is real and what is an illusion. If you veer towards illusions then something could dissolve in front of your eyes.

123

Tuesday 24th

You will be wanting to act on your fantasies. Talking about them with another gives you the urge to make them real. Take heed from the last few days that all that glitters is not gold, and see things and people for what and who they really are.

Wednesday 25th

Are you projecting your ideals onto others? If people start to disappoint you then you probably are. Building castles in the sky is the same as making sandcastles. Very soon they will come crumbling down and leave you wondering why you made the effort.

Thursday 26th

The Moon meets Mars today and you can feel victimised or blocked in your plans. Take some time out today before aggression builds and go and do something physical. Just spending time alone with a good book or TV show might ease the tension and keep you safe.

Friday 27th

There could be some issues in your love life today. Beware of volatile and selfish behaviour. You may experience some nasty surprises if you insist on provoking someone who holds an opposing point of view. Power struggles and control issues can be settled if you see both sides.

Saturday 28th

You need the larger group around you today. You want someone to agree with you and have the same philosophies as you. You do not want to stand out in the crowd as being wrong about something. You want to gather an army of support around you.

Sunday 29th

Today is an easier day than of late. You will know that only a Taurus can best meet their own needs by indulging in a little luxury or having a spending spree. Conversations are pleasant and the day goes quite smoothly. Enjoy this better atmosphere while you can.

Monday 30th

A full Moon in your money sector will ask you to take a good look at what you have and what you need. You could be in two minds about this and will struggle to see if there is anything that you actually just do not need. Let it go, Taurus.

DECEMBER

. . . .

Tuesday 1st

Today Mercury enters your house of sex, death and rebirth with an enquiring mind that wants your thoughts about recent issues. Do you want to talk about it? You may feel like sharing your thoughts with someone special.

Wednesday 2nd

You may be a busy little bull today. You will have lots of little tasks to do and many people to see. Sharing news and gossip with siblings or catching up with messages will be the theme of the day. Nothing spectacular will happen, but things will get done.

Thursday 3rd

Your mood is not in line with your drive today. You could feel a bit stuck in the mud and unable to get things moving. This may only be in your thinking, so today is the perfect day to relax and wallow in your dreams, visions and fantasies.

Friday 4th

You could get a little creative today and have some fun with it. Family surround and encourage you. Remember to act from the heart today and not from the ego, as your underlying mood just wants to be centre of attention. Play nice.

Saturday 5th

If you act with good intentions today and see a job to its conclusion, you could expect a reward. Be careful though, because Uranus in your sign can bring surprises or nasty shocks. It all depends on the energy you are putting out there to begin with.

Sunday 6th

You may want to assess the past and future with regards to where you have come from and where you would like to go. It is okay to dream about future plans, but do remember how things worked out for you in the past and do not repeat mistakes.

Monday 7th

Be good to yourself today as the Moon in your leisure sector may leave you feeling exhausted. Do only what is necessary and leave extras alone for today. Pencil in some fun time that will uplift you and make you feel buoyant and joyful.

Tuesday 8th

Positive and easy-going vibes will be sent towards your travel sector. Have you managed to find a way of combining work with your desire to explore? Use today to look again at this possibility. Your heart pulls you towards something new and you now see what you are able to do about it.

Wednesday 9th

Trying to find a balance between head and heart gets easier today, although you will still need to see what is illusion and what is reality. What is keeping you from seeing the truth? Take off the rose-coloured spectacles and see for yourself.

Thursday 10th

Do things that you can control today. Your ruler Venus is talking to Pluto who likes to use his power to change and control. He is also the ruler of Scorpio, your opposite sign, so this could mean that these issues are around your partner.

Friday 11th

Relationships from the past might come back, so prepare for these as they could bring up some issues that you have long forgotten about. They may also reveal the reasons why you behave as you do in significant relationships. Is this something that still serves you?

Saturday 12th

The Moon meets Venus in Scorpio today so there could be more issues surrounding past or current partners. Mars is also making you dream of past love and comparing this to what you have or what you want now. Some things are best left in the past, however. Time to move on now.

Sunday 13th

You are still thinking about partners past and present. You may also be thinking about finances that you have lost. On the other hand you may be thinking about investing and sharing something valuable with your partner or someone else important to you. Seek some wise advice first.

Monday 14th

A new Moon in your sex, death and rebirth sector sits right on top of chatty Mercury so you can talk about what has been on your mind recently. You have a chance to talk about money too. This comes easily to you but maybe not to others, so be tactful.

Tuesday 15th

Venus moves on and now sits in your sector described above. She will help you transform outdated patterns and habits and make something shiny and new from them. Love can go up a level and also down to some deep places that you never knew existed.

Wednesday 16th

Who is in control now? Has someone or something captured you so tightly that you have surrendered to their grip? This could be an idea, a plan or a person with whom you are enamoured now. Try to stay grounded and dig those hooves in. You do not want to lose your grip on reality.

Thursday 17th

Big things are happening for you, and you are being swept away with the current. First your mood turns to expansion and you have great joy and big plans, but then you seem to be knocked back into moodiness and feel limited. This is the Moon talking.

Friday 18th

You just cannot get a grip on your monkey mind today and that is because Mercury is absent without leave in your sex, death and rebirth sector. Have a quiet day today and switch off with some fantasy reading or viewing. Do not overtax your brain today.

Saturday 19th

There could be some tension today as Jupiter is on the last degree of your travel sector. It feels like you are waiting for the green light. Meanwhile, the Moon drifts into your social sector so this would be a good time to go out with friends.

Sunday 20th

The tension gets bigger today and almost tears you apart. You have a lot of nervous energy and do not know how to use it. Jupiter and Saturn are sitting together at the beginning of your career sector and having a board meeting. This will be the decider for your future.

Monday 21st

It's the shortest day of the year and here you are waiting for results from Jupiter and Saturn. The tension is electrified by the Sun and Mercury now entering your travel sector. This is looking good, so stay real and leave the celebrations until later.

Tuesday 22nd

How much longer can you hold this tension? The Moon now passes into your dreams sector and allows you to indulge in some fantasy. What are your wildest dreams? Do you want to keep them to yourself for a little longer or share the love?

Wednesday 23rd

Today it might feel like everything is going against you. Mars the warrior in your dream sector is squaring off with Pluto the transformer in your travel sector. These are co-rulers of Scorpio, your opposite sign, so you could look at your shadow and see where you are sabotaging yourself.

Thursday 24th

The Moon enters your sign on Christmas Eve and you will tend to over do it on all the seasonal goodies. It is the holidays and so you deserve it, but do not turn it into a selfish moment and end up as the fatted calf for tomorrow's dinner.

Friday 25th

Happy Christmas Taurus! If you did not go to excess yesterday then today you will be bouncing all over the place like a small child. If you did, then that is another story. You will be lurching around like a bull in a china shop. Slow down, it's Christmas!

Saturday 26th

It is the morning after the morning after and you just want to sit and watch some old movies. Do that, because it is just the thing to recover from what has been a year of nail-biting tension and pent-up frustrations.

Sunday 27th

Today you will be looking with satisfaction at your Christmas gifts. You will be checking your bank balance and making a note to deal with it in the new year. For now, you are happy to enjoy the remainder of the holiday season with family and friends.

Monday 28th

Already you are considering what the new year will bring and making resolutions. You might surprise yourself with what you come up with. You could be quite selfish today and not in the mood for love, but do not trouble your loved ones as this mood will pass soon.

Tuesday 29th

The last Full Moon of the year lands in your sector
of short trips and messages late in the day. Is there
anyone you need to catch up with before the festive
season ends? This Moon will highlight the need for you
to always check in with your loved ones and keep the
family bonds of love.

Wednesday 30th

The Moon opposite Mercury today means that your
head and heart will have a small battle and you will be
torn between family and career. You will be looking at
where your home is and the home you have created for
yourself. This can be a floaty day for you.

Thursday 31st

A mixed end to the year. The Moon is at home and wants
you to be too. You do not have the energy to argue with
anyone or to be the one in charge. Enjoy the last day of
2020 and have a good time reminiscing about what the
year has taught you.

Taurus

....

PEOPLE WHO
SHARE YOUR SIGN

PEOPLE WHO
SHARE YOUR SIGN

Ambitious Taureans dominate in their professional
fields, and their tenacity has seen many rise to fame
throughout history and in the present day. From famous
singers like Adele and Ella Fitzgerald, to top models
such as Gigi Hadid and renowned artists like Salvador
Dalí, the beauty that Taureans bring into the world is
evident. Discover the creative Taureans who share your
exact birthday and see if you can spot any similarities.

April 21st
Jessey Stevens (1992), James McAvoy (1979), Steve Backshall (1973), Iggy Pop (1947), Queen Elizabeth II (1926), Charlotte Bronte (1816), Robert Smith (1959), Diana Darvey (1945)

April 22nd
Louis Smith (1989), Tyra Sanchez (1988), Jack Nicholson (1937), Glen Campbell (1936), Queen Isabella I of Castile (1451), Immanuel Kant (1724), Daniel Johns (1973), Michelle Ryan (1984)

April 23rd
Gigi Hadid (1995), Taio Cruz (1985), Jaime King (1979), Shirley Temple (1928), Dorian Leigh (1917), Sandra Dee (1942), Michael Moore (1954), John Cena (1977), Kal Penn (1977), U.S. President James Buchanan (1791), William Shakespeare (1564)

April 24th
Casper Lee (1994), Joe Keery (1992), Kelly Clarkson (1982), Shirley MacLaine (1934), Austin Nichols (1980), Cedric the Entertainer (1964), Barbra Streisand (1942)

April 25th

Joslyn Davis (1982), Renée Zellweger (1969), Hank Azaria (1964), Al Pacino (1940), Len Goodman (1944), Ella Fitzgerald (1917), Oliver Cromwell (1599), Tim Duncan (1976), Alejandro Valverde (1980)

April 26th

Channing Tatum (1980), Melania Trump (1970), Kevin James (1965), Roger Taylor (1949), Jemima Kirke (1985), Luke Bracey (1989), Giancarlo Esposito (1958), Carol Burnett (1933)

April 27th

Patrick Stump (1984), Froy Gutierrez (1998), Jenna Coleman (1986), Darcey Bussell (1969), Tess Daly (1969), U.S. President Ulysses S. Grant (1822), Coretta Scott King (1927)